Fall Colors

of

Ouray

A Photo and Coloring Book

Margaret Henderson

Dedication

For anyone who enjoys the splendor of fall in the mountains.

Photographs by Margaret Henderson

Front Cover: Road to Silver Jack Reservoir

The photographs in this book as well as others of the Ouray area may be purchased by contacting:

Margaret Henderson

http://www.ouray.biz
P.O. Box 590
Ouray, CO 81427

Contents

Preface

Fall in Ouray brings breathtaking mountain views amidst leaves turning gold, orange, red, brown and gray. Whether a sunny or cloudy day, the glorious colors of fall infiltrate the air, coloring your view and your disposition. The hint of winter to come is subtle, but a present reminder that the fleeting days of the golden splendor are to be savored as the hours and minutes go by. Preserving them in photographs is a joy of capturing the turning of colors moment by moment. The brilliance and gradations of the colors creates special opportunity for coloring -- blending colors and drawing faint outlines of veins of leaves or serrated edges of foliage.

In this picture and coloring book, I have provided the photograph as the scene appeared the day it was taken and an outline for you to color the picture as it was that day or as you imagine it might have been before, a few shades lighter, or later as the colors saturated over the course of time. Use the photos and outlines for your drawing pleasure and inspiration.

Use your creativity and imagination and enjoy the splendor of fall in and around Ouray!

Fall Colors of Ouray is the second book in a series about Ouray. The first, *Ouray 365: What It is Like to Live in Ouray All Year Round*, describes life in Ouray. One of the benefits of living in Ouray year round is being able to enjoy the fall season, watching the colors change daily in all weather conditions.

Mount Sneffels

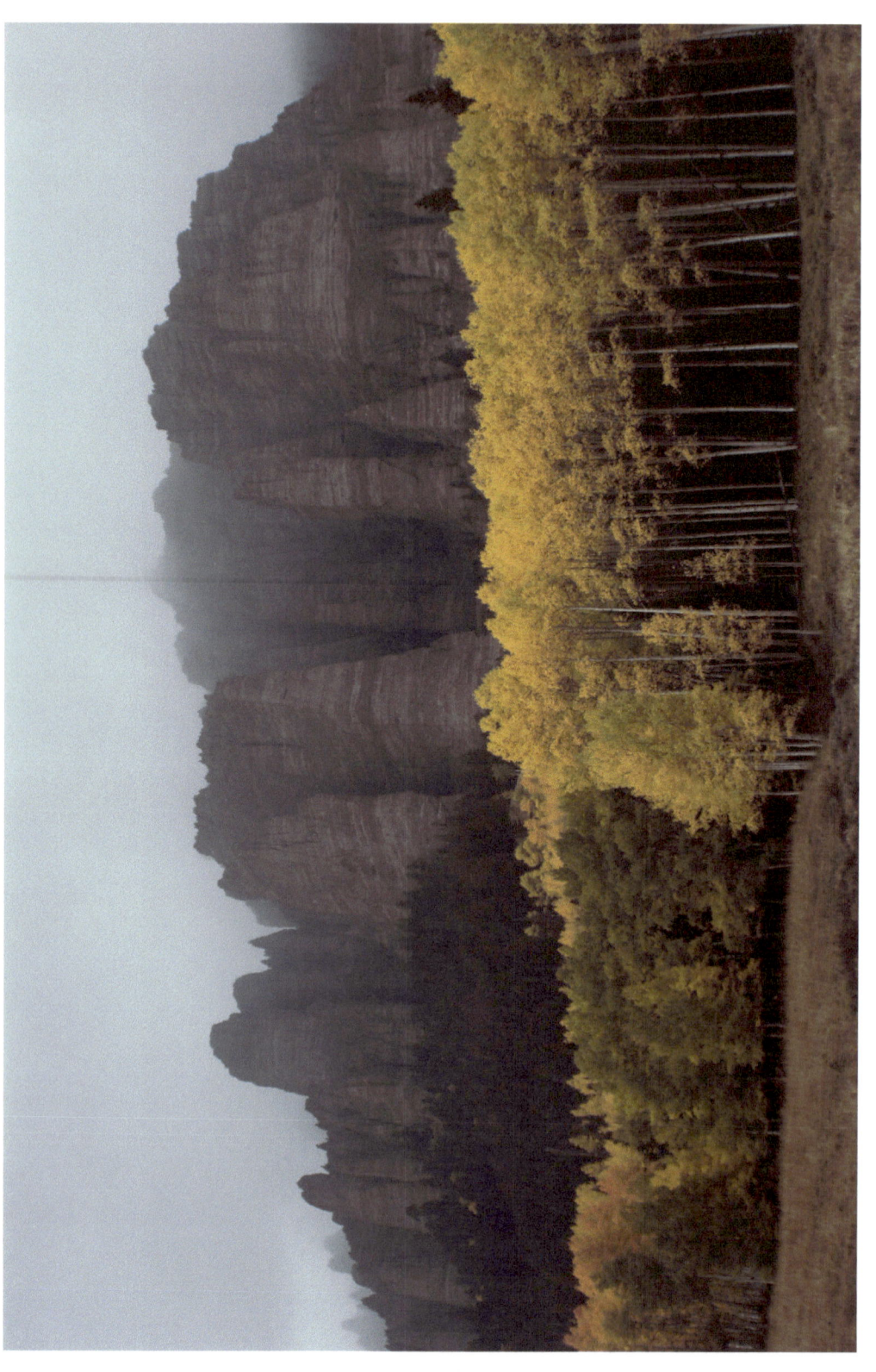

Owl Creek in Fog

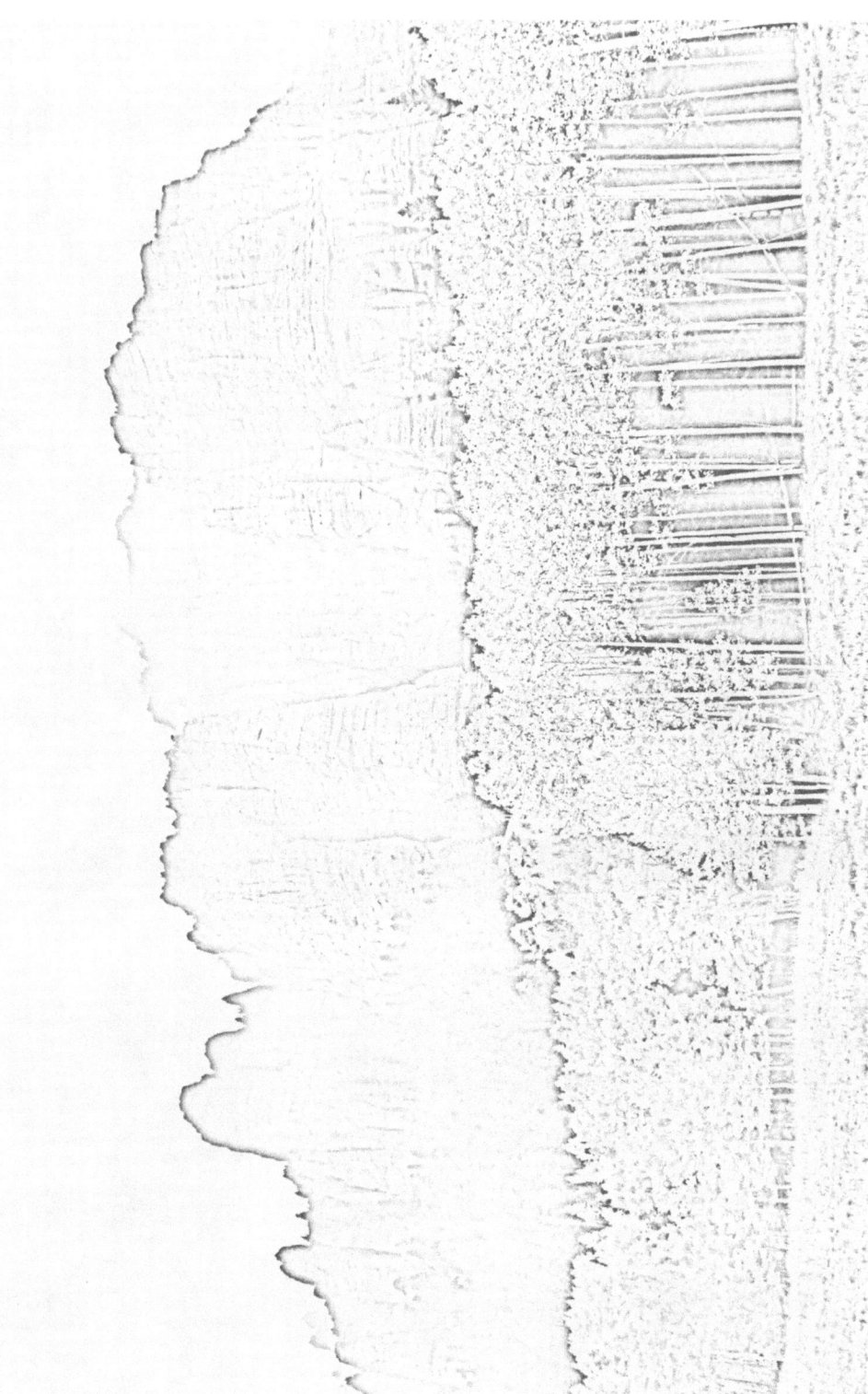

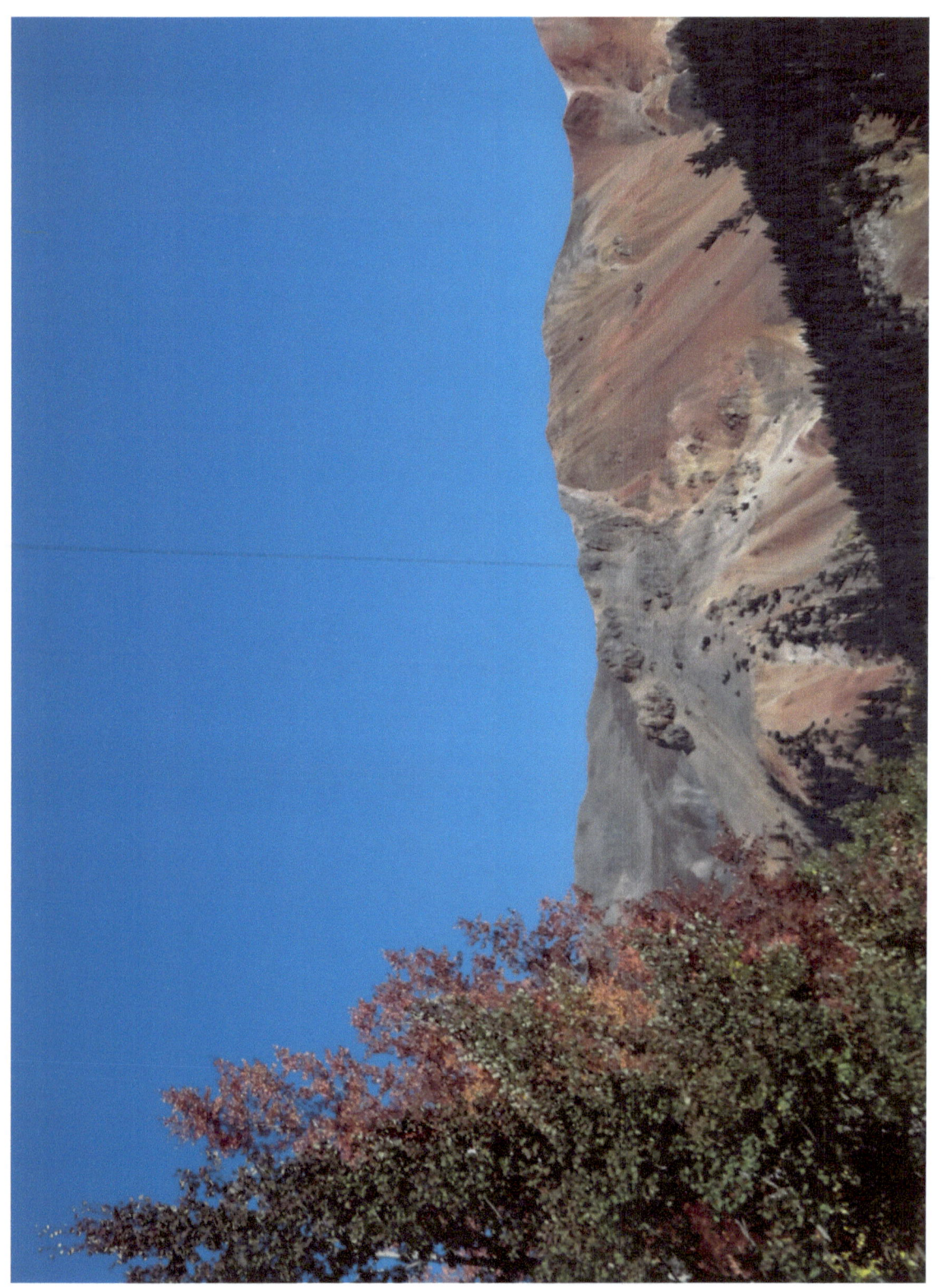

Red Mountain

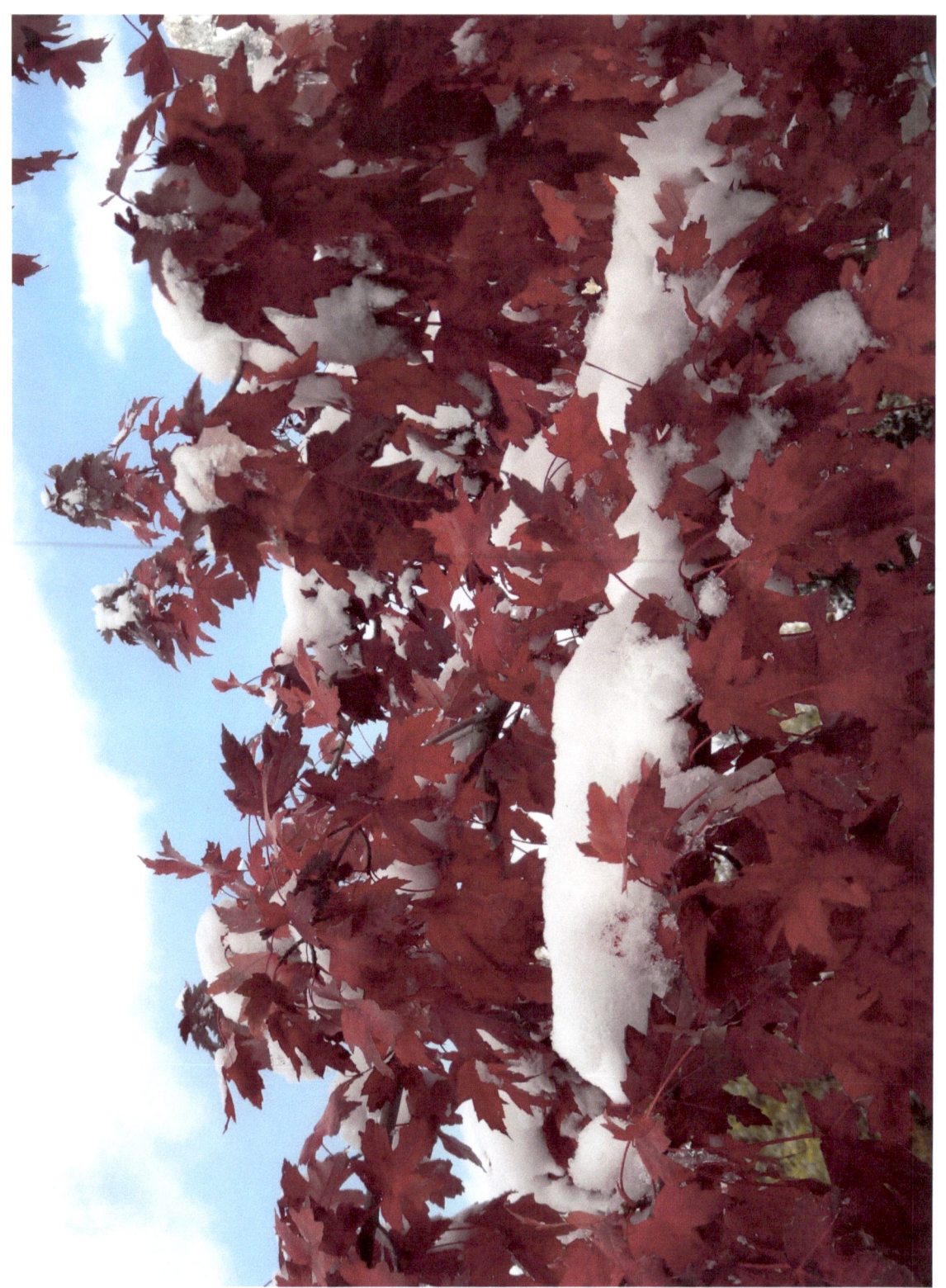

Maple Leaves

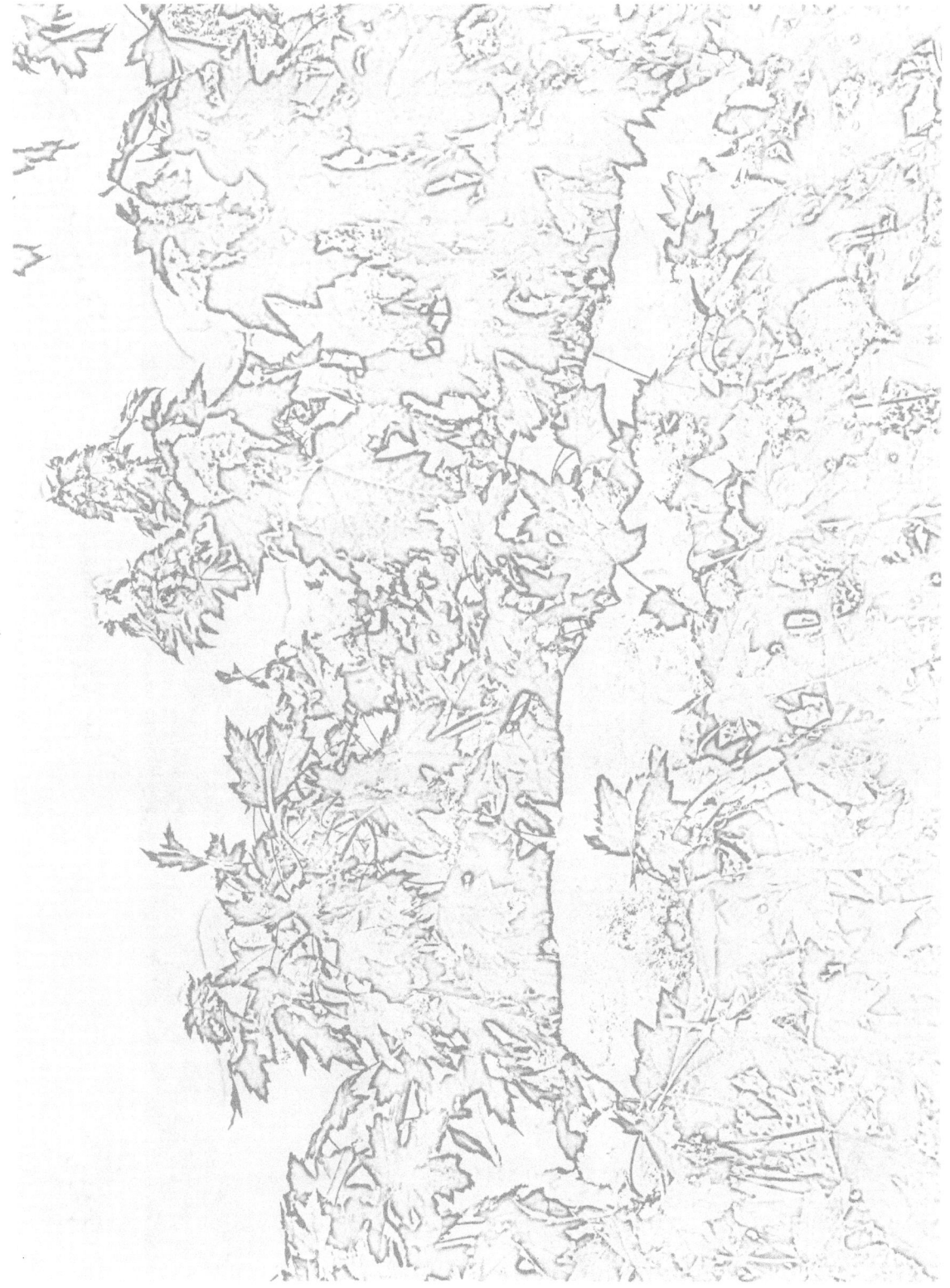

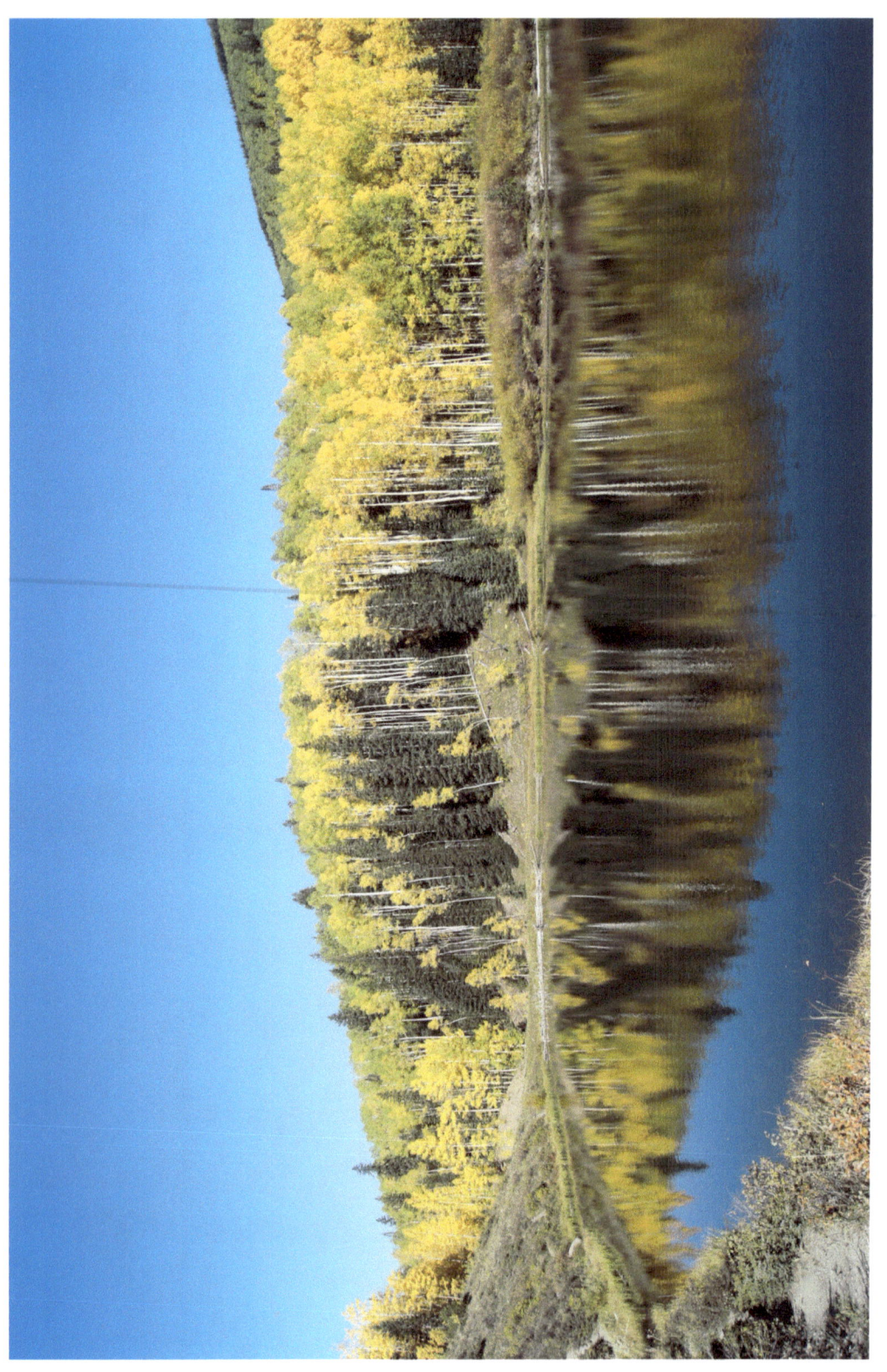

Woods Lake

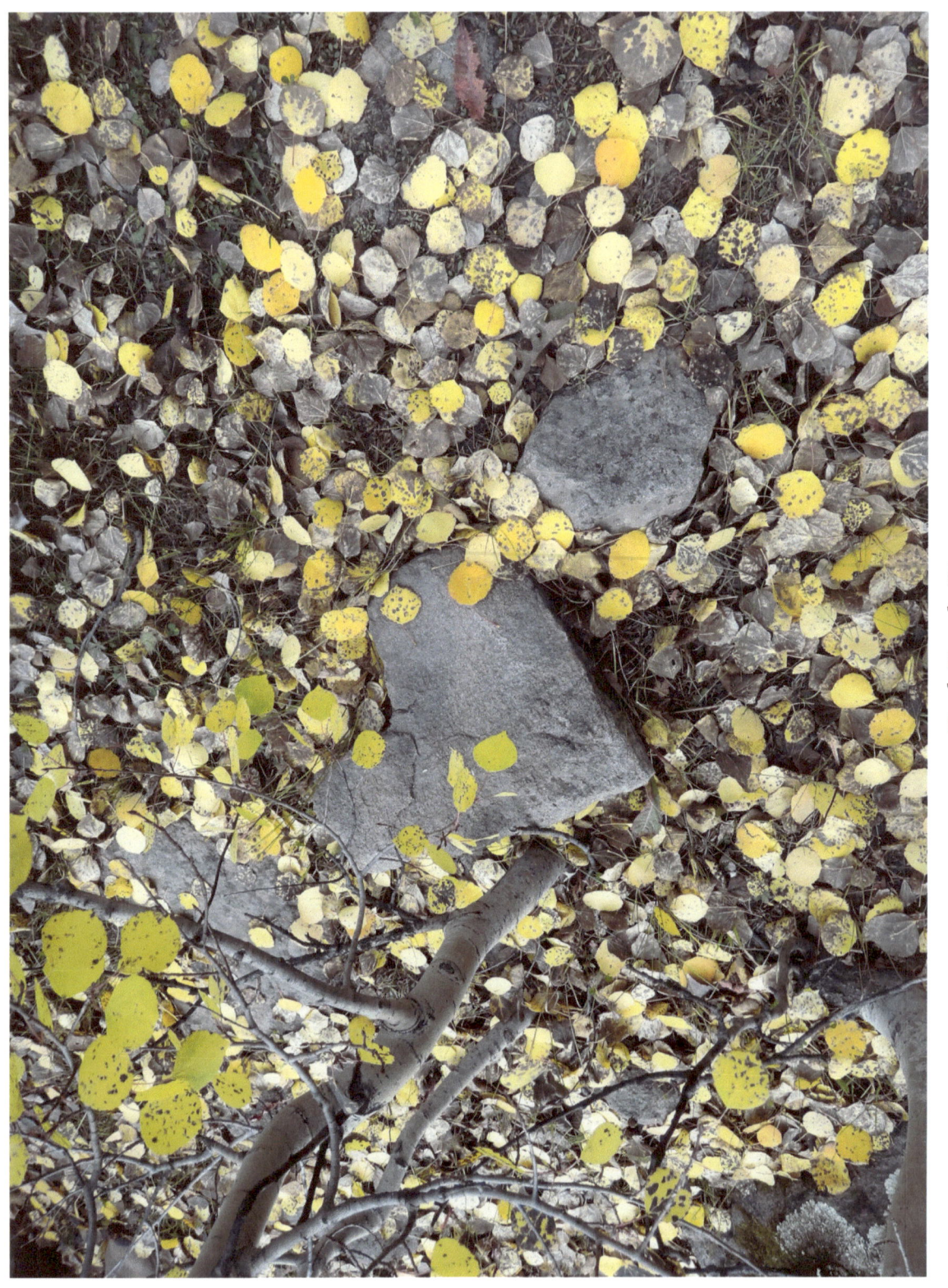

Owl Creek Heart

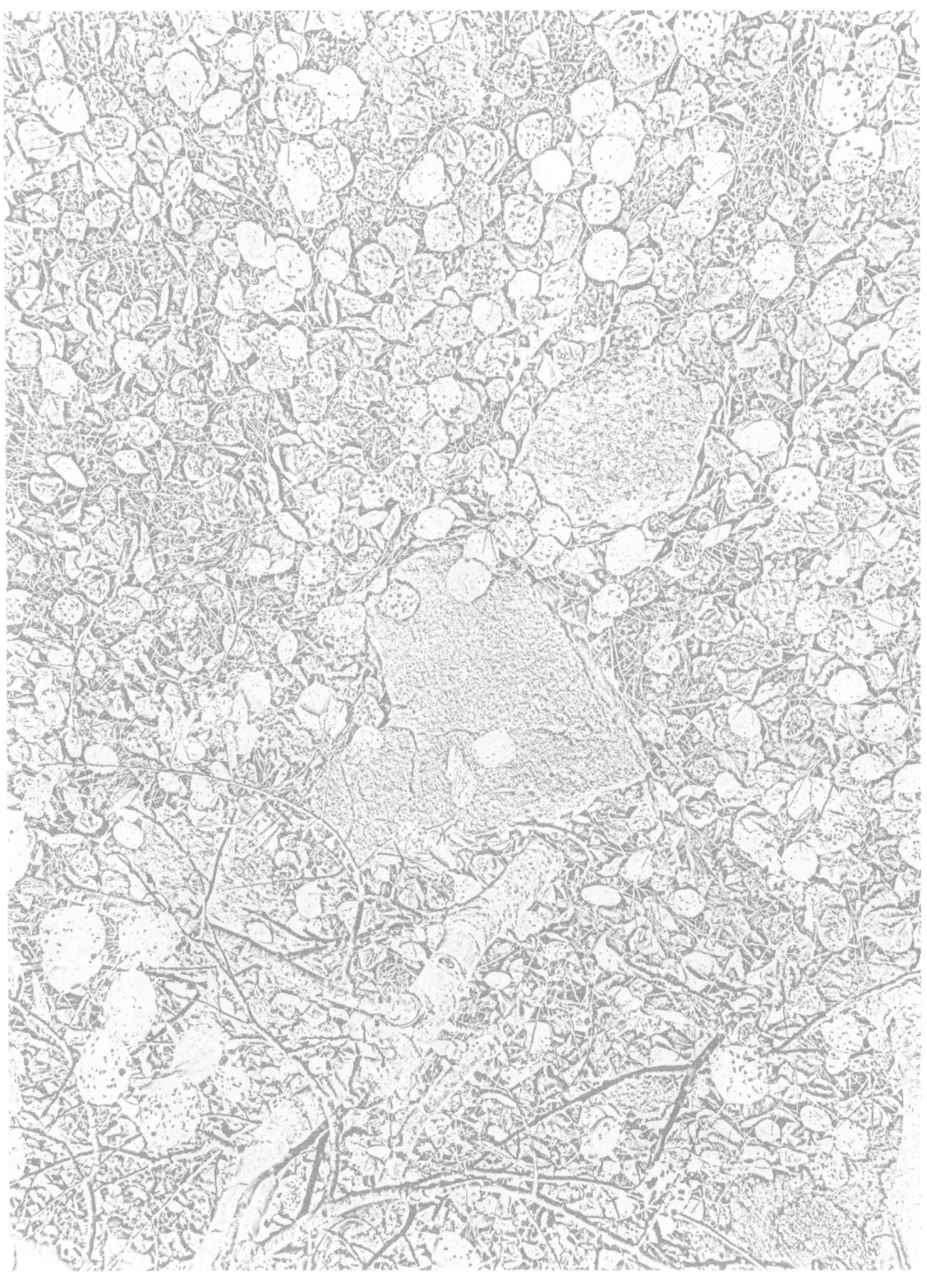

West Elk Loop

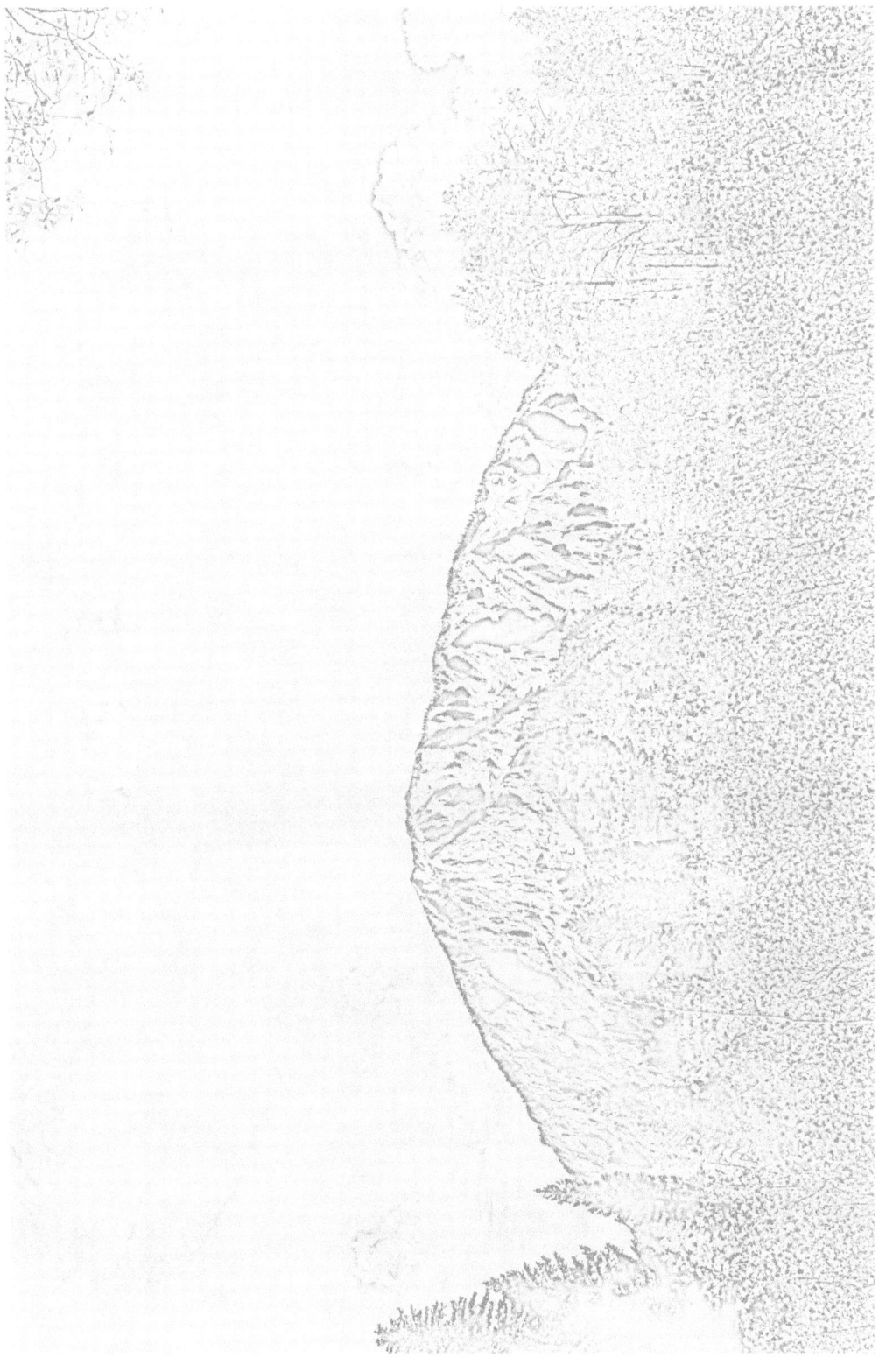

Aspen Turning

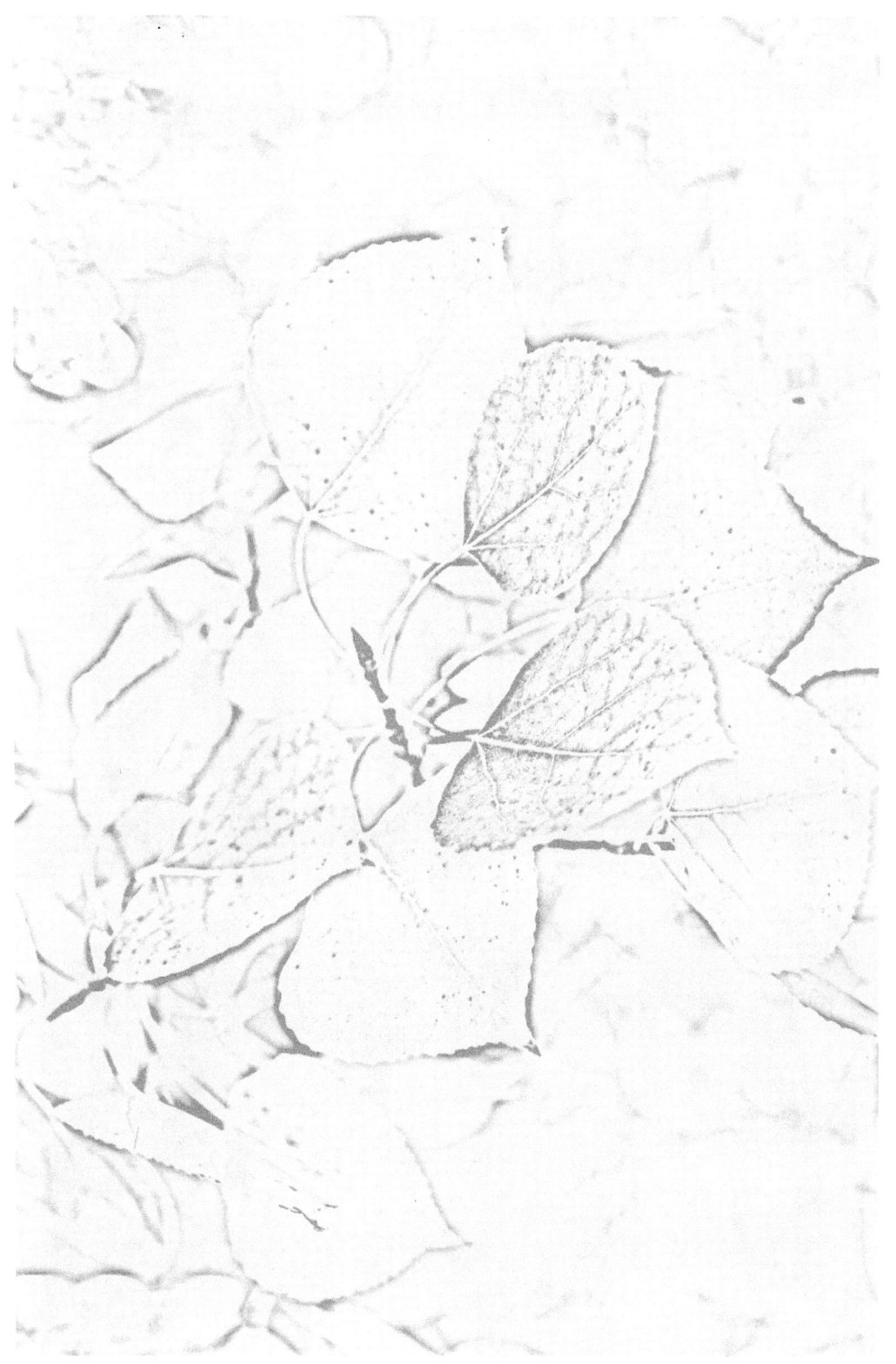

Road to Silver Jack Reservoir

Road to Buckhorn Lakes

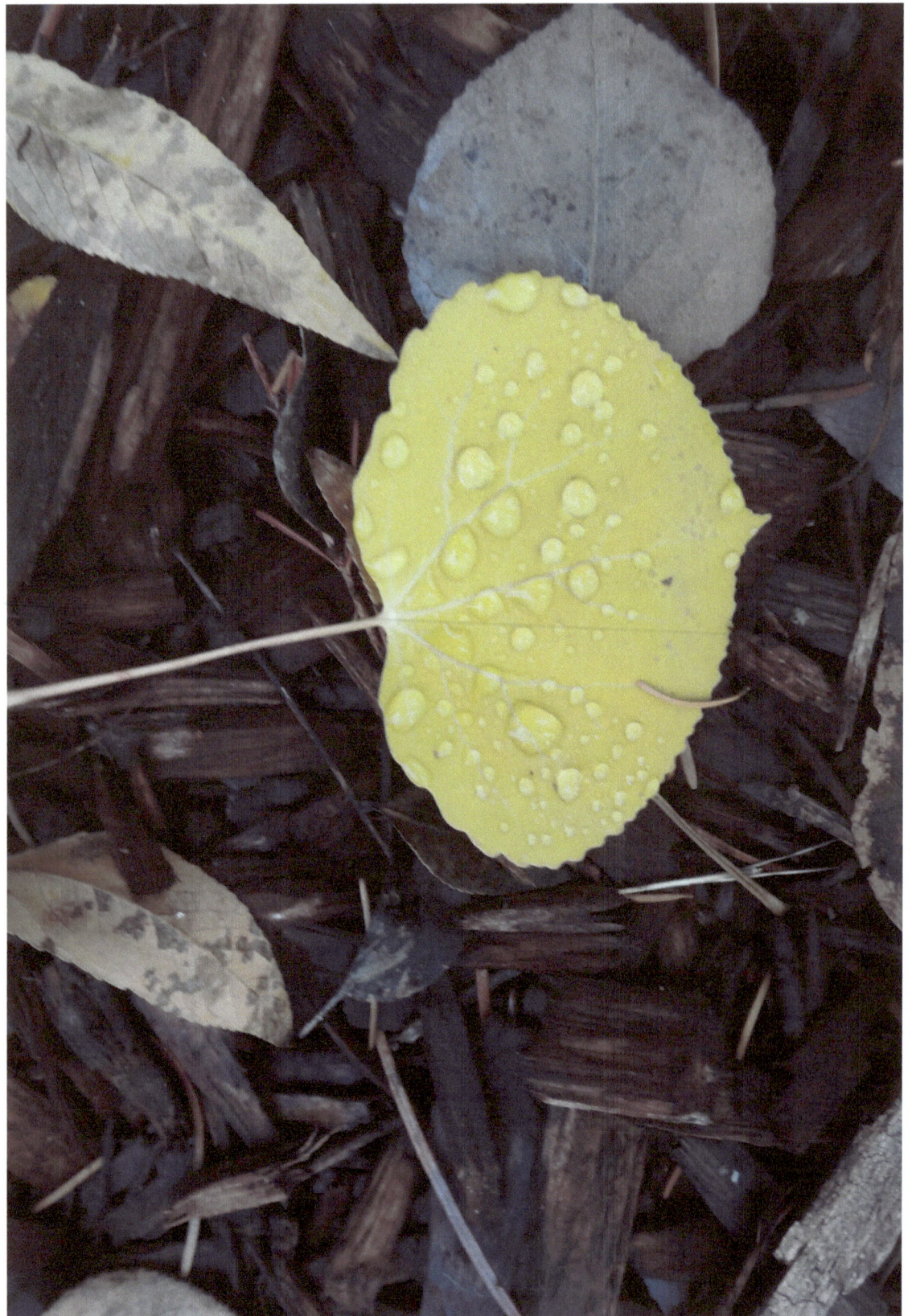

Aspen Leaf

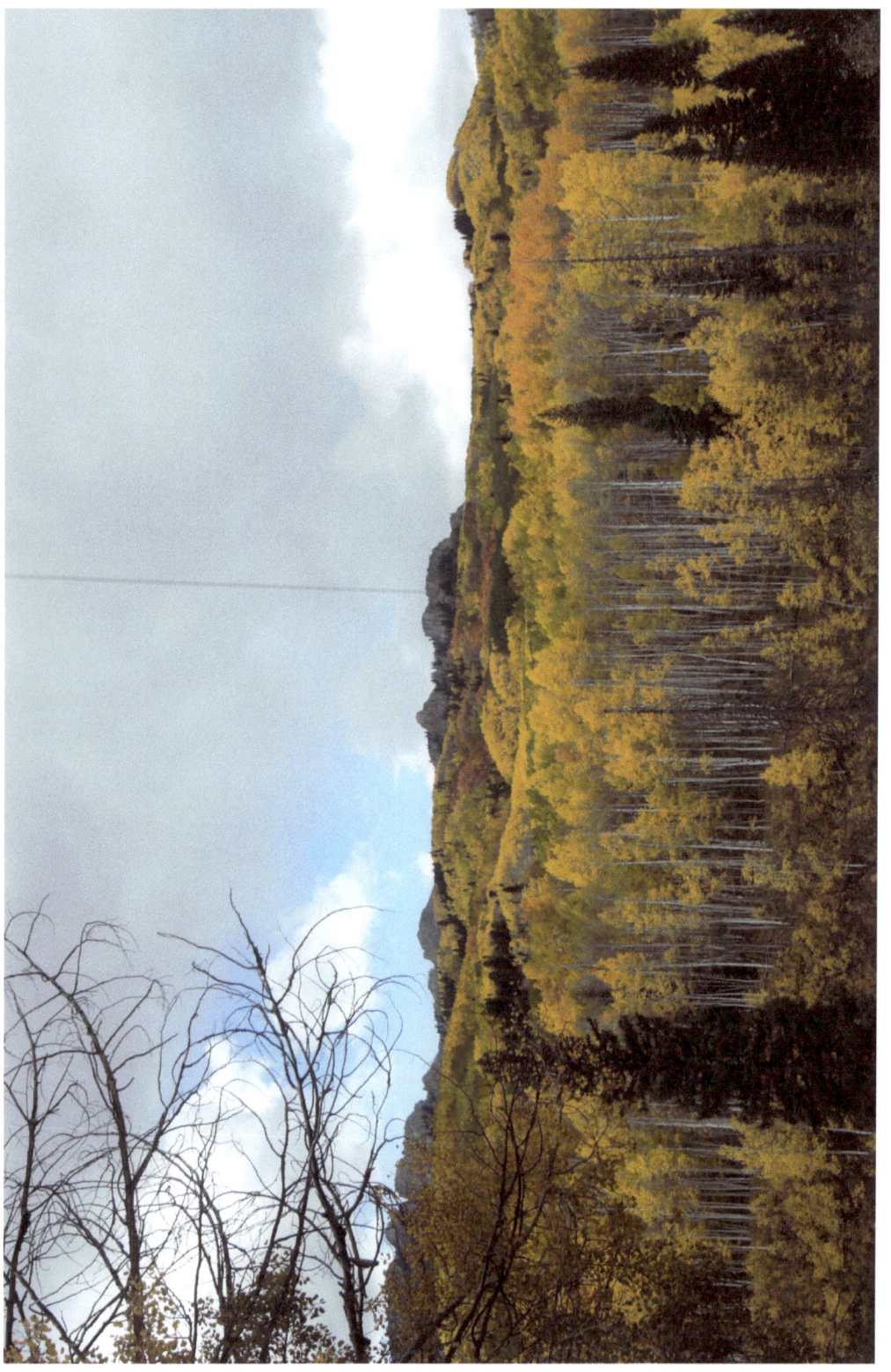

West Elk Mountains

Grand Mesa Overlook

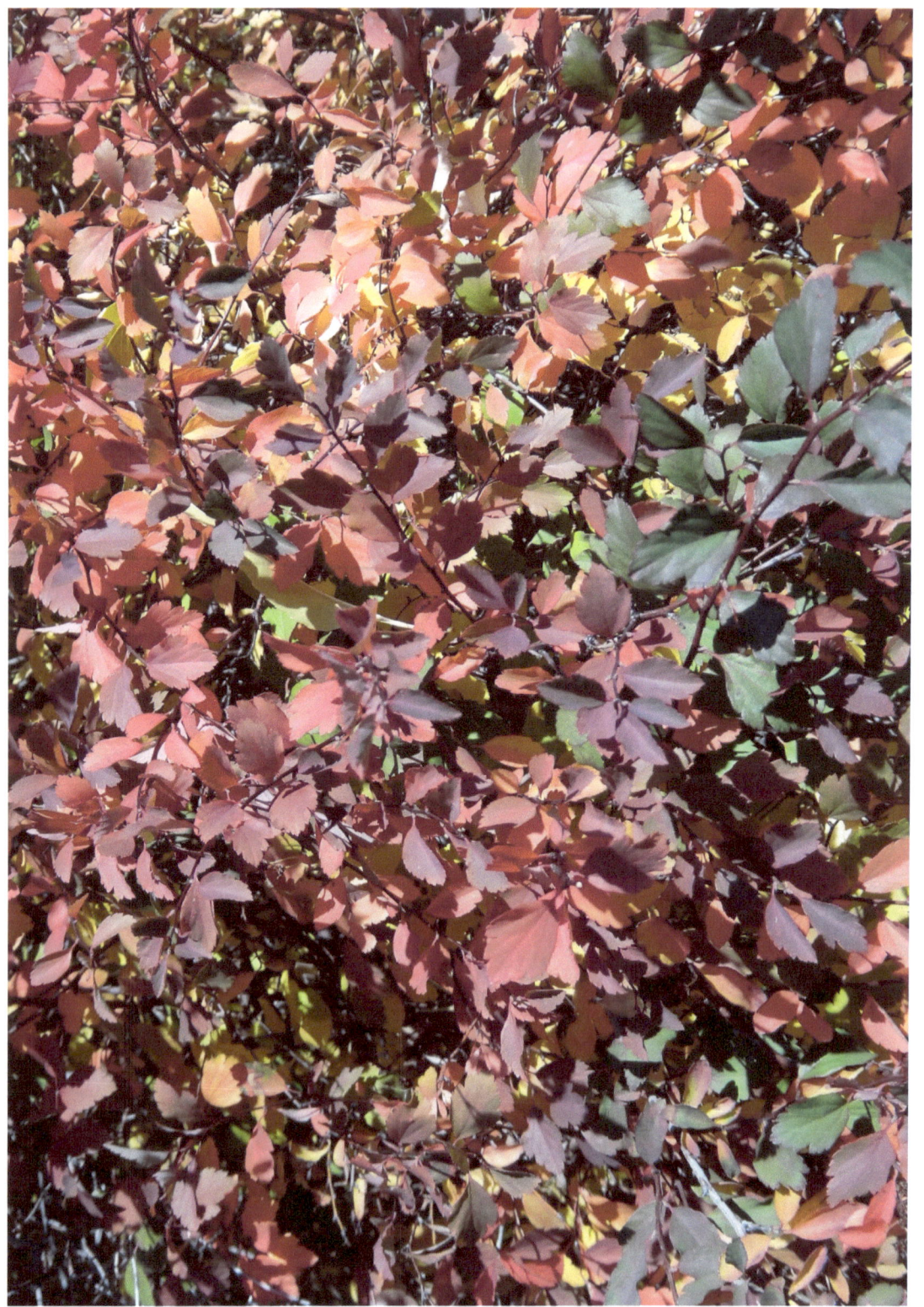

Lilac Leaves

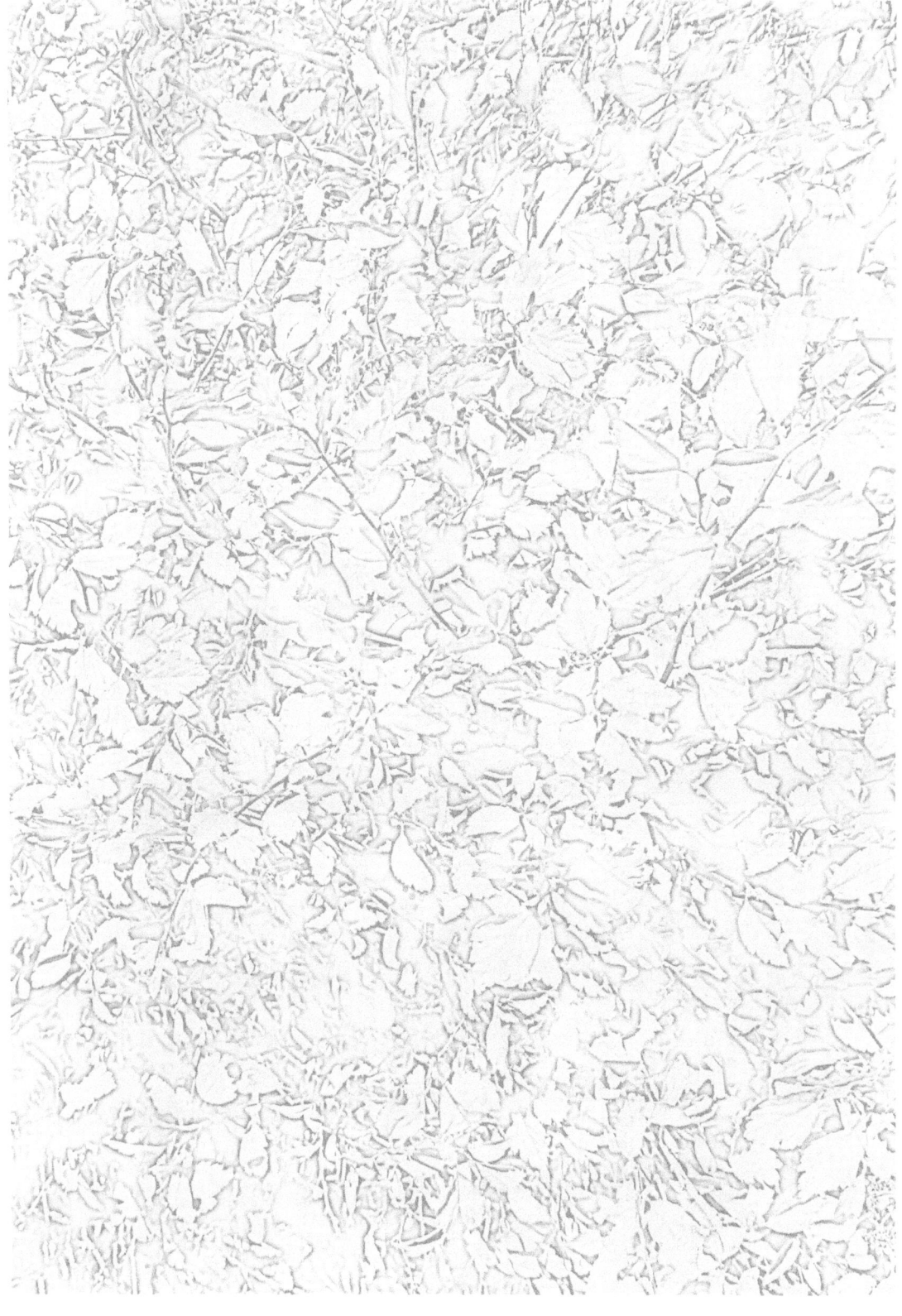

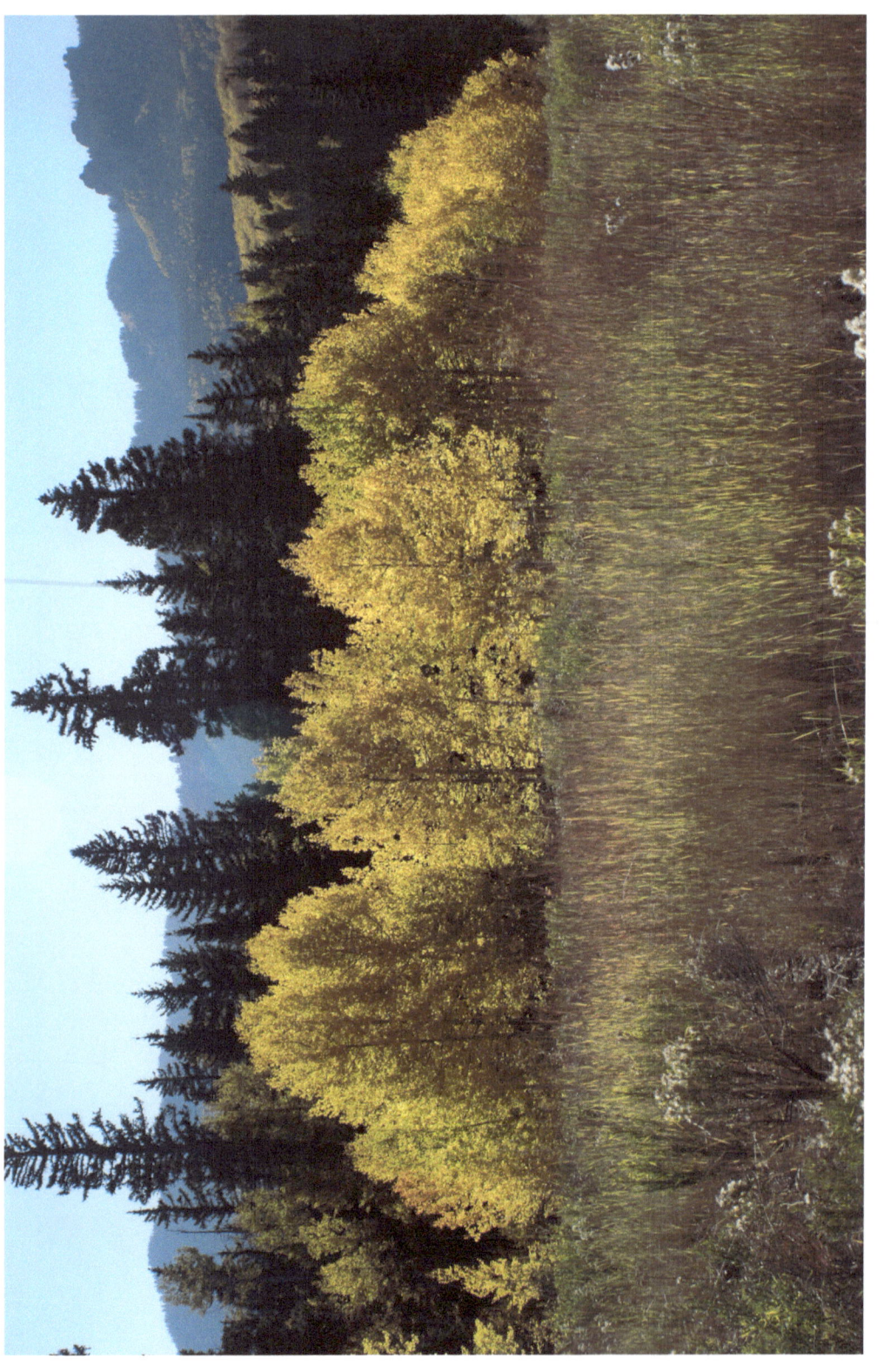

Mountain Views

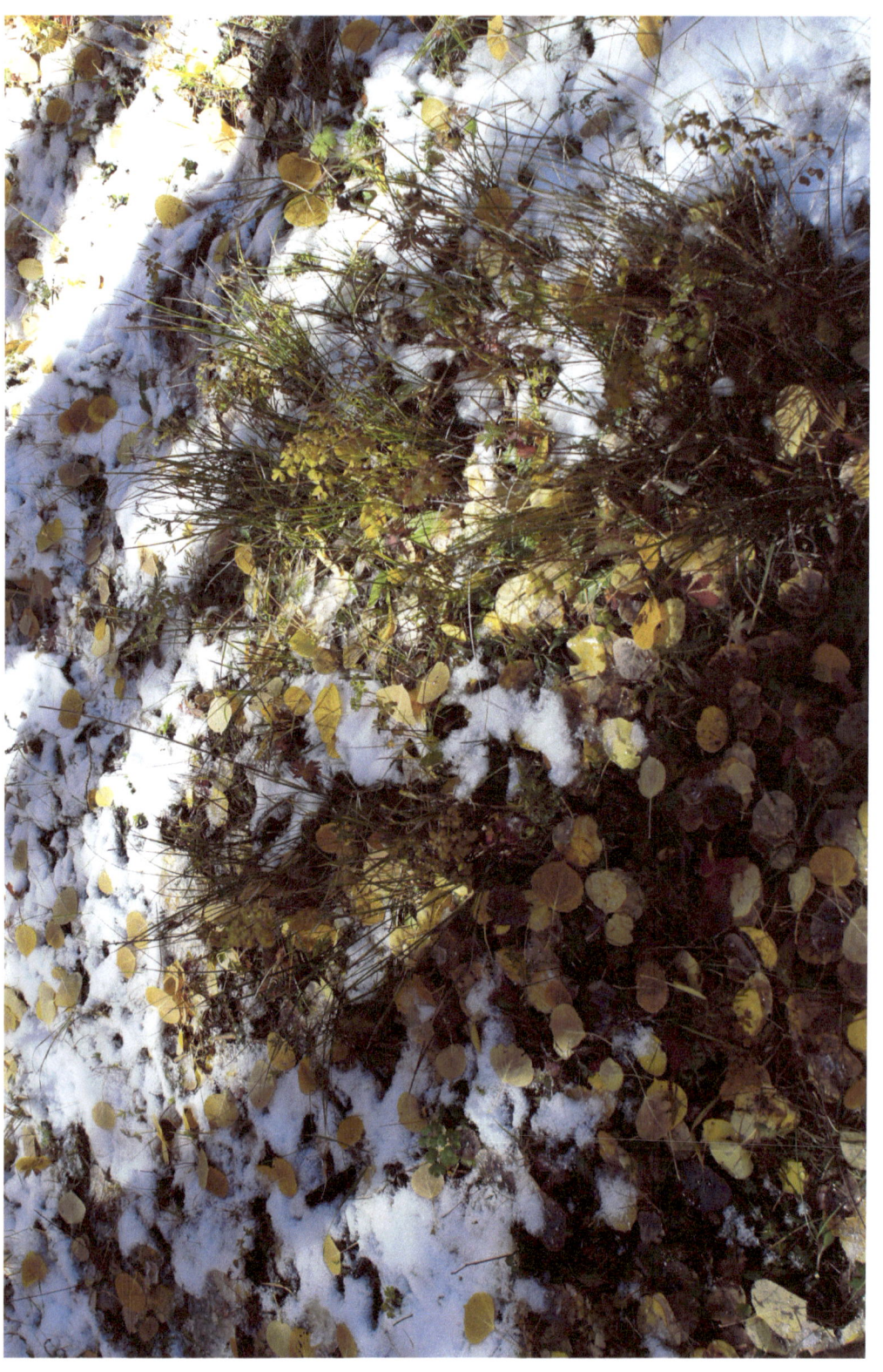

Leaves in Snow

My Fall Colors

www.ingramcontent.com/pod-product-compliance
Lightning Source LLC
Chambersburg PA
CBHW051104180526
45172CB00002B/772